Warthogs

Victoria Blakemore

vblakemore.author@gmail.com

Copyright info/picture credits

Cover, Tom Strudley/Shutterstock; Page 3, lizv/Pixabay; Page 5, AlamaCreative/Pixabay; Page 7, jpussin/Pixabay; Page 9, THIERYFLAMAND/Pixabay; Pages 10-11, EcoView/AdobeStock; Page 13, Darilon/Pixabay; Page 15, IanZA/Pixabay; Page 17, kyslynskyy/AdobeStock; Page 19, tonyo_au/Pixabay; Page 21, Atilla JANDI/AdobeStock; Page 23; IanZA/Pixabay; Page 25, emt244671/Pixabay; Page 27, nike159/Pixabay; Page 29, mattyh/Pixabay; Page 31, Dawie Jacobs Photography/ Shutterstock; Page 33, Tom Strudley/Shutterstock

Table of Contents

What Are Warthogs?

Warthogs are large mammals.
They are members of the
swine family. Other members
of the swine family include
boars, pigs, and hogs.

Warthogs get their name from
the large bumps on their
heads. The bumps look like
large warts.

Warthogs are usually brown, tan,

black, and red in color. The color

of their skin and fur can help

them blend in to their habitat.

Size

Warthogs are usually between three and five feet long. They stand over two feet tall at the shoulder.

When fully grown, warthogs often weigh between one hundred and three hundred pounds.

Male warthogs, or boars, are

much larger than female

warthogs, or sows.

Physical Characteristics

Warthogs have tusks on their snouts. Their tusks are actually large teeth. They can be used for self defense.

They have very little hair. The hair they do have is thick and **coarse**. They also have a mane along their back.

All warthogs have bumps on their heads. The bumps are usually largest on boars. The bumps are hard and can protect them in a fight.

Habitat

Warthogs are usually found in grasslands, savannas, and forested areas. They prefer areas with lots of plants for them to eat.

It can be very dry where warthogs live. They tend to stay near a water source such as a lake or river.

Range

Warthogs are usually found
south of the Saharan desert
on the continent of Africa.

They are often found in countries like Botswana, South Africa, and Zambia.

Diet

Warthogs are **omnivores**. They eat both meat and plants.

Their diet is mainly made up of plants like grasses, fruits, berries, and roots. They can also eat insects and small mammals.

Warthogs spend a lot of their time

grazing for grass. They sometimes

eat soil for the **nutrients**.

Staying Cool

It can be very hot where warthogs live, so warthogs have a special way to keep cool. They roll around in the mud.

The mud helps to keep them cool. It also works as a sunscreen and can keep the bugs off of their skin.

When warthogs spend time in
the mud, it is called wallowing.
Other animals that wallow
include pigs and rhinos.

Communication

Warthogs use mainly sound and movement to communicate with each other.

They can make sounds such as squeals, grunts, snorts, and growls. A lot of these sounds are used between sows and their piglets.

When warthogs run, their tail stands up. This can be used as a warning to other warthogs that danger is nearby.

Movement

Warthogs have long legs for their size. This allows them to be fast runners. They can run over thirty miles per hour when needed.

They are very flexible. They can bend their front legs and kneel to reach the ground.

Warthogs have been seen
shuffling around in the kneeling
position when they are eating.

19

Burrows

Warthogs live in burrows that are dug in the dirt. However, they don't usually dig the burrows. They live in old burrows that aardvarks dug.

The burrows are usually large with long tunnels. They provide warthogs with a safe place to sleep.

When warthogs leave their

burrows, they run out quickly.

They do this in case a predator

is waiting outside.

Warthog Piglets

Warthogs usually have two or three babies. Their babies are called piglets. They are born in a burrow.

Piglets stay close to the burrow. If they are **startled**, they quickly dive back in. They may share a burrow with other sows and piglets.

Sows protect their piglets from predators when they are little.

They can protect themselves after about two years.

23

Warthog Life

Sows and their piglets live in groups called sounders. Boars are usually more **solitary**.

Warthogs often have problems with bugs biting them. There are several kinds of birds that sit on warthog backs and eat the bugs. This helps the warthogs and the birds.

Warthogs are most active during the day. In places where they are hunted, they may be more active at night when it is safer.

Population

Warthogs are not **endangered**.

There are many left in the wild.

However, in many areas,

warthog populations have

been **declining**.

In 2014, there were **estimated**

to be about 22,000 warthogs in

the wild.

In the wild, warthogs often live

between eight and thirteen

years.

Warthogs in Danger

In many places, warming temperatures have caused **droughts**. This makes it difficult for them to find food and water.

Warthogs can carry diseases that make **livestock** sick. Some people kill warthogs to protect their animals.

Some people hunt warthogs for their meat, skin, and tusks.

Helping Warthogs

In many places, special protected areas have been set up. They provide animals such as warthogs with a safe habitat to live in.

These protected areas can also be wildlife **corridors** that help animals get from one safe place to another.

Some groups are working to teach people about warthogs. They want to help people find ways to live close to warthogs without killing them.

Other groups are trying to learn more about warthogs. They want to learn more so we can find new ways to help them.

Glossary

Coarse: rough, not soft

Corridor: hallway or passageway

Declining: getting smaller

Drought: a long period of time with little or no rain

Endangered: at risk of becoming extinct

Estimated: come to from a careful guess

Grazing: eating grass

Livestock: animals such as sheep, pigs, and cows that are kept by humans

Nutrients: something in food that helps people, plants, and animals to grow

Omnivore: an animal that eats plants and animals

Solitary: living alone

Startled: scared, frightened

About the Author

Victoria Blakemore is a first grade

teacher in Southwest Florida with a

passion for reading.

You can visit her at

www.elementaryexplorers.com

Also in This Series

Also in This Series

Aardvarks	Mako Sharks	Alligators	Frogs	Hedgehogs	Brown Bears	Bongos
Sea Turtles	Quokkas	Muskrats	Zebras	Red Foxes	Ring-Tailed Lemurs	Platypuses
Anteaters	Kangaroos	Rhinos	Jaguars	Wombats	Capybaras	Gorillas
Cats	Skunks	Butterflies	Dingoes	Snow Leopards	African Wild Dogs	Penguins
Whale Sharks	Wolverines	Warthogs	Caracals			

All books by Victoria Blakemore